TD - 13 - 05 - B1

T2 - AJY - 802

EXPLORING THE SCIENCE OF NATURE

The Nature and Science of

REFLECTIONS

Jane Burton and Kim Taylor

Gareth Stevens Publishing
A WORLD ALMANAC EDUCATION GROUP COMPANY

Please visit our web site at: www.garethstevens.com
For a free color catalog describing Gareth Stevens Publishing's list of high-quality books
and multimedia programs, call 1-800-542-2595 (USA) or 1-800-461-9120 (Canada).
Gareth Stevens Publishing's Fax: (414) 332-3567.

Library of Congress Cataloging-in-Publication Data

Burton, Jane.
The nature and science of reflections / by Jane Burton and Kim Taylor.
p. cm. — (Exploring the science of nature)
Includes bibliographical references and index.
ISBN 0-8368-2194-7 (lib. bdg.)
1. Reflection (Optics)—Juvenile literature. [1. Reflection (Optics).]
I. Taylor, Kim. II. Title.
QC381.6.B87 2000
535'.323—dc21 00-030766

First published in North America in 2001 by
Gareth Stevens Publishing
A World Almanac Education Group Company
330 West Olive Street, Suite 100
Milwaukee, Wisconsin 53212 USA

Gareth Stevens editors: Barbara J. Behm and Heidi Sjostrom
Cover design: Karen Knutson
Editorial assistant: Diane Laska-Swanke

Printed in the United States of America

1 2 3 4 5 6 7 8 9 05 04 03 02 01

Contents

Words that appear in the glossary are printed in **boldface** type the first time they occur in the text.

Types of Reflections

In most cases, objects become visible when they **reflect** light. Light bounces off smooth, shiny surfaces in one direction. Light bounces off rough surfaces in many directions.

When a mirror or the smooth surface of water reflects light from the Sun, the Sun's reflected **image** becomes visible. When a flower reflects sunlight, however, the Sun is not visible in the flower because the rays of light bounce off in every direction. If the flower did not reflect light, it would not be visible at all. Instead of a flower, we would see a black, flower-shaped hole.

A leaf in summer reflects some colors strongly, but it reflects other colors only slightly. A leaf does not reflect much red or blue light, but it reflects a lot of green light. That is why the leaf looks green.

Light is not the only thing in our world that is reflected. If you shout loudly in certain locations, the sound of your voice may bounce off objects. This reflected sound is called an **echo**. If you throw a stone into a pond, the stone makes ripples. The ripples travel to the edges of the pond and bounce off, forming a pattern of reflected ripples. Heat and **radio waves** are reflected in a similar way to light, but these waves are not visible to the naked eye in the same way that light is visible.

Above: A red harlequin butterfly strongly reflects red and blue light.

Opposite: The shiny, smooth surface of Crater Lake in Oregon reflects an upside-down image of the mountains.

Below: The head of a green iguana is mirrored in the still waters of a pool.

Mirror Images

A mirror reflects light in a special way. For example, **rays** of light that reflect off a cat and then strike a mirror are reflected together in the same direction. The cat is then able to see its image in the mirror. The surface of a mirror is flat and very smooth. It needs to be; otherwise the image will be **distorted** or there may be no image at all. The surface of a lake can act as a mirror if there are no ripples. The slightest ruffling of the surface will make the image break up or disappear.

Right: Although this cat's right paw nearly touches the water, the reflected image of the cat makes it seem as though its left paw is nearest the edge of the pond.

Left: Reflections of poplar trees appear upside down on the surface of a lake.

Looking at an object's image in a mirror is not the same as looking at the object directly. Hold this book up to a mirror, and you will see that the image is reversed. Similarly, trees growing at the edge of a lake leave upside-down reflections in the water. A cat's real right paw looks like its left paw in a reflected image.

Mirrors work according to the law of reflection. Light rays that strike a mirror are reflected at exactly the same angle as they struck the mirror. The ray of light that strikes the mirror is called the incident ray. The ray of light that leaves the mirror is the reflected ray.

Above: This male fairy wren notices its image in a car mirror. It attacks the image, thinking the reflection is another male fairy wren.

Right: In the middle of the day, when the Sun is high in the sky, most of the light striking the surface of water passes into the water. These gouramis and tiger barbs, swimming over pebbles and water plants, are clearly visible from beneath the surface of a tropical pool.

Below: When light from the evening Sun strikes the surface of the water, most of it is reflected. Hardly any light enters the water. The bottom of this stream is so dark that the heron probably cannot see any fish.

The shiny surface of a mirror reflects all light regardless of whether the light comes from the side or directly from the front of the mirror.

No light can pass through a mirror. The surface of water is different. Some light is reflected from the surface of a pond, and some passes through to the bottom. How much passes into the water depends on the angle at which the light strikes the surface of the water. When light strikes water at **right angles**, most of the light passes into the water, and just a small amount is reflected. When light strikes at a much more narrow angle, nearly all of the light is reflected.

For instance, a bird searching for food in the water has the best chance for success in the middle of the day when the Sun is high in the sky. In the evening, most of the Sun's light is reflected from the water's surface, leaving the bottom in darkness.

The view from beneath the surface of the pool is quite different than from above. The water's surface still transmits and reflects light. Beyond a certain angle, however, all the light is reflected. A fish looking up from below the surface of the water sees the sky and any trees that surround the pool as a wide circle. Outside this circle, all light is reflected, and the fish sees only reflections of the bottom and sides of the pool. No light is transmitted, and the surface acts as a perfect mirror.

Left: These carp are reflected on the underside of the water's mirrorlike surface as they come to the surface to eat. When viewed from below at a narrow angle, the surface of a pond forms a perfect mirror.

Imperfect Images

Top: The reflected image of this great blue heron seems wavy because of ripples on the surface of the water.

A mirror is a perfectly flat, shiny surface. A shiny surface that is not perfectly flat can reflect an image, but the image is distorted. The image is stretched out, squeezed in, or even broken into several pieces.

Look at reflections in a pond on a day when there is a gentle breeze. Reflections of trees or houses in the pond will appear wavy or broken up by ripples. Because the surfaces of the ripples are

Top: The reflected image of this great blue heron seems wavy because of ripples on the surface of the water.

Right: Ripples on the surface of this lake make zigzag reflections of a northern pintail.

Left: Although the Moon itself is hidden behind a tree, its reflection forms a pathway leading up from the horizon.

Below: A gleaming pathway of reflections leads from the surface of the sea to the rising Moon.

not flat but have many different angles, light from any one direction is reflected at many angles. This causes the image to break up and distort.

Imagine a full Moon rising over a choppy sea. Light from the Moon comes straight into your eyes, and the Moon looks perfectly round. Light from that same Moon reflected in the choppy water, however, does not form this same image. The reflection appears as a lovely, shimmering pathway leading up to the Moon. The waves reflect the moonlight in all directions, and the pathway is formed by millions of ripples.

Scattered Light

Top: This harlequin bug reflects blue, green, orange, and yellow colors while absorbing other colors.

A white chalk cliff reflects just as much of the Sun's light as a mirror, but no image of the Sun can be seen in the cliff. This is because a mirror has a shiny surface, and the cliff has a **matte** surface. The rough surface of the chalk reflects the Sun's rays in all directions. The reflected light is **scattered**. Snow, like chalk, also reflects most of the light that falls on it. It forms a white blanket that can be so bright that it is blinding. Most of the light reflected from snow is scattered, but occasionally, flat snow crystals form tiny mirrors that reflect unscattered light from the Sun. The crystals make freshly fallen snow sparkle brilliantly in the sunlight.

Right: The chalk boulder in the foreground reflects and scatters most of the Sun's light. The surrounding darker pebbles **absorb** most of the light.

Left: Snow appears white in color because it reflects all colors and absorbs none. Snow has a matte surface, so the light reflected from it scatters.

Clouds and smoke also reflect scattered light, but they do not reflect all the light that falls on them. Some light passes through. On a cloudy day, light still reaches the ground. The Sun's light is scattered on its way through the clouds.

Above: Ice crystals on snow contain flat, shiny surfaces that act like mirrors to reflect the Sun's light directly. These tiny "mirrors" make the snow sparkle brilliantly.

Left: Sunlight passing through these clouds is scattered. Beneath the clouds, the scattered light appears soft and produces no shadows.

13

Scattered light is normal on Earth. Rocks, plants, and animals scatter light when they reflect it. Only the surface of water and a few shiny objects, such as fish scales, do not scatter light. The amount and nature of the light reflected from different objects are different, however.

Many objects absorb the light of some colors and reflect the light of others. For instance, a red berry strongly reflects red light but absorbs the light of other colors. A brilliantly colored butterfly

reflects some colors but absorbs many others. Only reflected colors are visible to the human eye. Snow reflects all colors equally and, therefore, looks white. Coal absorbs all colors and, therefore, looks black.

The surface of the Moon consists of gray dust and rocks that scatter the Sun's light in all directions. A bright Moon is actually reflected sunlight. At night, the Moon is so bright that it appears to be giving off its own light, like a sun.

Light rays from the Moon run nearly side by side or **parallel** by the time they reach Earth. Moonlight is again scattered when it reflects off of rocks on Earth.

Left: The surface of the Moon seems like a gray desert. At night, people see sunlight reflected off of it but call that sunlight "moonlight."

Top: The reverse
image of a tree in
this raindrop was
not reflected. It was
formed by refraction.

Reflections in Raindrops

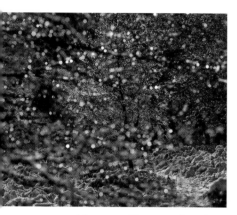

Above: Drops of water
formed from melted
snow split the Sun's light
into colors. The colors
are visible in any one
drop for a brief moment
when the angle of the
Sun is just right.

Right: Refraction allows
you to see this terrapin's
left front foot in two
places — through the
surface of the water
and through the side of
the tank. The terrapin's
head is reflected in the
surface of the water.

Light from the Sun appears to have no color.
Sunlight is, in fact, made up of light from all the
colors of the rainbow mixed together. People see
this mixture of colors as white light. Colorful
objects lit by the Sun absorb some colors and
reflect others. When white light from the Sun
shines on a raindrop, the light is bent at an angle
by the surface of the drop. The light bends again as
it passes out of the drop. The bending of light
when it passes from air to water, or from water to
air, is called **refraction**.

Each of the colors in sunlight is refracted at a slightly different angle. Red light is bent the least and violet light the most. A rainbow appears when thousands of raindrops separate all the different colors of light from the Sun.

Rainbows form as a result of more than just refraction. As sunlight enters a raindrop, the light separates into colors. The colors are then reflected by the mirrorlike inside of the drop in a process called total internal reflection. Refraction separates the colors even more when they leave the drop.

Look for a rainbow on a day that is both sunny and rainy. When you see the rainbow, the Sun will always be behind you. Rainbows seem to curve because you see half of a circle of sunlit drops that are at the same angle from your eyes.

Above: The rainbow in the spray from this waterfall in Iceland is formed when sunlight is refracted and then reflected by tiny water drops. Beneath the rainbow, white light is reflected toward you. Above the rainbow, no light is reflected toward you by the spray.

Echoes

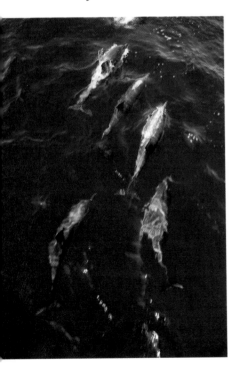

Top: This serotine bat sends out ultrasonic squeaks from its mouth. The bat finds its way around by listening for echoes from the squeaks.

Below: Dolphins direct beams of ultrasound forward. The echoes that bounce back reveal to the dolphins what objects lie ahead.

Sound reflects in the form of echoes. Sometimes echoes are distorted, and they no longer resemble the original sound. For instance, a handclap or a shout in a cave results in a ringing echo that continues for a second or two. The **sound waves** scatter in all directions because they bounce off the rough walls of the cave. This bouncing produces a ringing sound.

Not all sound waves behave in this way. Many animals and insects produce sounds that are too high pitched for humans to hear. Similar to light waves, these **ultrasonic** sound waves travel in straight lines and can be directed into a beam. Bats, dolphins, and certain other animals use the echoes of their own ultrasonic squeaks to find their way around in darkness or muddy water where light does not penetrate.

The system used by these animals is known as **echolocation**. A bat or dolphin makes a short squeak or click and then listens for an echo. Any object in the path of the squeak reflects the sound back toward the animal. By noticing the amount of time that passes between the squeak and the echo, the animal can tell where the object is. From the type of echo, the animal can even tell the nature of the object in its path — whether it is rough or smooth, solid or hollow, hard or soft. The animal may even be able to tell if there is another object inside a hollow object.

Sound travels at 770 miles (1,240 kilometers) per hour in air and much faster in water. Because of this high speed, animals using echolocation must accurately judge very short time intervals. As an example, when a bat is flying among the numerous branches of a tree, it has to squeak so often that its squeaks become a continuous buzz.

Below: This pipistrelle bat must squeak many times a second and listen for the echoes to avoid flying into these twigs.

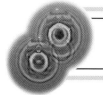

Reflected Ripples

Top: Rings of ripples reflect the impact of two drops of water falling into a pool.

Sound consists of **pressure waves** in air, water, or even solid materials. A sound wave is produced when an object vibrates rapidly back and forth. **Molecules** of air around it are pushed together, **compressing** the air. There is no sound in outer space, at least that humans can hear, because there is no air. Light consists of **electromagnetic waves** for which space is no barrier at all. Ripples on the surface of water are yet another kind of wave.

All these kinds of waves have two things in common: they travel in straight lines, and they can be reflected. Ripples on a pool of water bounce off any solid object, such as a rock or log. The direction in which the reflected ripples travel

Right: Light consists of electromagnetic waves that can travel through space. Light from the comet and stars shown here traveled millions of miles (km) through space to reach Earth.

20

depends on the angle at which the incoming ripples strike the object. Ripples on water act the same way that light does when it strikes a mirror. Reflected ripples leave a flat object at the same angle at which they originally struck the object.

Drop two stones into a pool of water. The rings of ripples cross each other without affecting each other. Sound waves and most kinds of light waves also pass through each other without any effect.

Below: Two drops of water fall onto the surface of a pool, forming two rings of ripples.

Below: As the two rings of ripples expand, they pass through each other with no effect on each other.

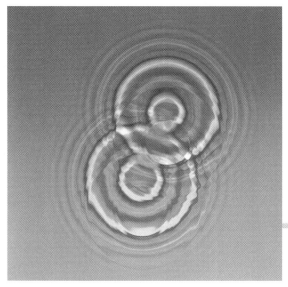

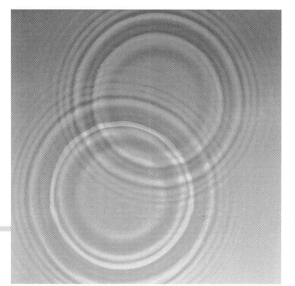

Eyeshine

Top: The tawny owl has very big eyes to help it see in the dark.

Some animals see in the dark much better than people can. A cat prowling around at night sees well enough to catch a mouse. Animals that hunt at night have eyes that are specially **adapted** to dim light — starlight, for instance.

One way in which **nocturnal** animals have adapted to low light is with the size of their eyes. Big eyes take in more light than small eyes, so nocturnal animals have big eyes.

Deep-sea creatures and nocturnal animals have adapted to low light in another way. They all have a silvery layer at the back of the eye, called a **tapetum**. The tapetum is located immediately behind a layer of light-sensitive **cells**, called the **retina**.

Tapeta cause some animals' eyes to shine brilliantly at night when the beam of light from a car's headlights lands on them. A tapetum reflects all the light that passes through the retina back to its source. The retina senses the light, both as it comes into the eye and again as it is reflected out of the eye. It receives a double dose of light. An eye with a tapetum sees twice as much in the darkness as an eye without a tapetum.

The human eye does not have a tapetum. Our eyes glow dull red from the light of a flashlight or a camera flash.

Opposite: A cat can leap and land on a fence in the dark of night. Each of a cat's eyes has a reflecting tapetum that helps the cat see in dim light.

Below: The eyes of many animals, including people's, reflect red. The red reflection in this wallaby's eyes indicates that it has no tapeta.

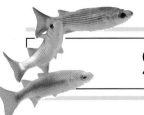

Silver Scales

Top: The silver sides of the gray mullet reflect the blue color of the water around them. Their gray backs do not reflect the bright sky.

An animal that is silver in color, like a mirror, is often easy for other animals to see — especially when the color reflects the bright sky. For most animals, therefore, silver is not a good **camouflage** color.

Many **species** of fish that live in open water, however, have silver scales. The scales reflect the color of the surrounding water so that the fish blend into the background and are hard for **predators** and other enemies to see.

Below: In artificial light from the side, angel fish gleam brilliantly.

Below: In natural light, angel fish reflect the color of their surroundings.

The reason the color silver works so well as camouflage for fish in open water is that, underwater, background color is always very much the same. This is true regardless of the direction in which an observer is looking.

A predator looking toward a silver fish sees just a dark blue background color with the same dark blue color reflected in the side of the fish. These fish also have dark, nonreflecting scales on their backs to prevent the bright sky from being reflected. Their dark backs hide the fish from predators that look down from above.

Although land animals are rarely silver in color, some butterfly **pupae** are partly or entirely silver. Their striking, shimmering appearance may be just a clever disguise, however. The pupae are motionless, so it is possible that predators simply might not realize that such glittering objects could actually be food.

Above: This pupa of a butterfly looks like polished silver. It is easy for predators to see, but it warns them that it may be poisonous.

Top: The glowworm is an insect that produces its own light. It is one of the few things in the natural world that does not rely on reflected light to be seen.

Mirages

It is easy to understand how the image of a bright sky can be reflected in a pool of water. It is more difficult to understand how a bright sky can be reflected in a pool of air, but this does happen under special conditions. When the ground is heated by the hot, midday Sun, the layer of air next to the ground also heats up and **expands**. As the air expands, it becomes less **dense**. The point between this less dense air and the denser, cooler air above refracts light. The light bends just a small amount so that rays from the sky appear to be reflected from the ground. The resulting image is called a **mirage**.

Mirages occur most often in the desert. They may appear silvery, like a distant lake reflecting the sky. As the observer gets closer to the mirage, the image melts away — leaving only hot, baking sand.

There are only a few living things on Earth that produce their own light. Living things depend almost entirely on reflected light to identify objects and get around. Reflected sunlight or artificial light makes objects visible. Living things exist in a world of reflections.

Above: These toadstools, called luminous fungi, reflect daylight in the jungle of Borneo.

Below: At night, they glow with their own light.

Opposite: Springboks live in the intense heat of the Namib Desert in Africa. Beyond them, an island of rock seems to float in a shimmering sea. The "sea" is not real — it is a mirage.

Activities:

Mirror Patterns

Mirrors can play tricks on your eyes. Look in a mirror, and you will see in front of you a room that is actually behind you. Peer into a mirror that is facing another mirror, and you will see a "tunnel of mirrors." Light bounces back and forth between the mirrors, creating the impression of a tunnel stretching a long way into the distance.

Several mirrors angled toward each other can produce fascinating patterns as the light bounces between them. A collection of mirrors that creates such patterns is called a kaleidoscope. Make one for yourself.

Make a Kaleidoscope
You will need three small rectangular mirrors, preferably without frames. You will also need tape and scissors (below).

Tape the mirrors together by their long edges to form a triangle of mirrors, all facing inward. When you tape the mirrors, one should be raised higher than the other two by about 3/4 inch (2 centimeters). This will leave a gap under this mirror when the kaleidoscope is placed on end.

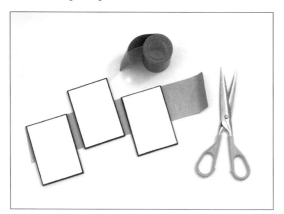

Stand the kaleidoscope on a flat surface so that the raised mirror is farthest from you. Put some small flowers, beads, or other colorful objects in the angle between the two mirrors nearest you. When you look into the mirror on the far side of the kaleidoscope, you can see a colorful pattern. The pattern always appears in the form of a six-sided star (below). The star is made of images of the same objects reflected one, two, and three times.

Make a Periscope
When you finish experimenting with your kaleidoscope, remove the tape from the mirrors. Use two of the mirrors to make a

periscope. The periscope will allow you to keep watch over the top of a bush or around the side of a building without being seen.

Basically, a periscope consists of a long tube with a reflecting mirror at each end. The reflecting surfaces are parallel to one another. They are arranged at a 45-degree angle inside the tube.

To make your own periscope, you will also need two 1-quart (1-liter) milk cartons, a knife, tape, a pencil, and a ruler.

Note: *If you do not have milk cartons, use ordinary cardboard or corrugated cardboard and the other materials shown on the next page to assemble your periscope (next page, left).*

Have an adult help you remove the top of each milk carton with a knife. You should now have tall, rectangular boxes.

Cut a rectangle a little less than the size of your mirror out of the bottom front of one of the milk cartons. Put the carton on its side with the top facing to the right. On the side that is now the topside, measure 2 3/4 inches (7 cm) up the left edge of the carton and

make a pencil mark. Draw a diagonal line from the bottom right corner to the mark. Use the ruler to make it straight.

With the knife, cut upward toward the left edge, starting at the bottom right corner. Make the cut only as long as the width of your mirror. Slide one of the mirrors into this slot and tape it in place. The reflecting side of the mirror should face the rectangular hole in the front of the carton.

Make the second milk carton identical to the first.

Place one of the cartons straight up on a table with the hole facing you. Stand the second milk carton on top of the first, upside down, with the mirror facing away from you.

You now have a periscope made of the two cartons. If you wish, you may connect the two cartons with tape to create one long tube. Now that your periscope is done, you can look into each of the mirrors to see over under and around objects.

When you use your periscope, notice the position of the image. You are looking at the reflection of a mirror image. An image that is reflected once is reversed. If the image is reflected twice, it is back to normal.

Strange Faces

Most animals' faces can be divided into two equal halves. The right and left halves are mirror images of each other. If an animal is partially under water, its above-water portion forms an image reflected in the water's surface.

Viewed together, the above-water part of an animal and the reflected image can look like the right and left halves of a brand-new, unusual animal.

Below: A common toad and its reflection seem to transform into a strange, extraterrestrial being.

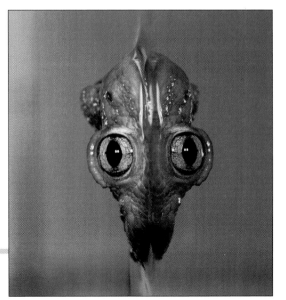

Glossary

absorb: to soak up radiation or liquid.

adapted: having made changes to better survive a situation or certain conditions.

camouflage: color or patterns on an animal that help the animal blend in with its surroundings.

cells: the microscopic building blocks of plant and animal bodies.

compressing: squeezing something into a smaller space.

dense: having a lot of mass per unit.

distorted: twisted out of shape.

echo: reflected sound.

echolocation: a means of navigation that makes use of sound and its echoes.

electromagnetic waves: the form in which heat, light, and other kinds of energy travel through space.

expands: gets larger and, therefore, occupies more space.

image: a picture.

matte: rough or nonreflecting.

mirage: the image that occurs when light is bent by layers of air that have of different densities.

molecules: the smallest units into which a substance can be divided and still keep the features of the substance.

nocturnal: active at night.

parallel: running side-by-side without getting closer together or farther apart.

predator: an animal that hunts other animals for food.

pressure waves: variations in force or thrust that travel through air or water, or even solid materials, to produce sound.

pupae: the stage in the development of insects before they become adults. *Singular: pupa.*

radio waves: electromagnetic variations that carry sound and television signals through space.

rays: beams of light or other forms of radiation.

reflect: to turn back or away.

refraction: the bending of light as it passes through material such as water.

retina: the layer of light-sensitive cells at the back of the eye.

right angles: the ninety-degree angles at the corners of a square or rectangle.

scattered: bounced in all directions.

sound waves: variations in pressure that produce sound.

species: a biologically distinct kind of animal or plant. Similar species are grouped into the same genus.

tapetum: a shiny layer behind the retina in the eye. The tapetum helps certain animals see in dim light. *Plural: tapeta.*

ultrasonic: referring to high-pitched sound frequencies, too high for humans to hear.

Plants and Animals

The common names of plants and animals vary from language to language and from place to place. Their scientific names, based on Greek or Latin words, are the same the world over. Each kind of plant or animal has two scientific names. The first name is called the genus, or generic name. It starts with a capital letter. The second name is the species, or specific name. It starts with a small letter.

angel fish (*Pterophyllum scalare*) — South America 24

common dolphin (*Dolphinus delphis*) — seas worldwide 18

Congo tetra (*Micralestes interruptus*) — Africa 25

cruiser butterfly (*Vindula arsinoe*) — Australia 14

glowworm (*Lampyris noctiluca*) — Europe 26

gray heron (*Ardea cinerea*) — Europe, Africa 8

gray mullet (*Mugil labrosus*) — Atlantic 24

green iguana (*Iguana iguana*) — South America 5

luminous fungi (*Filoboletus manipularis*) — Southeast Asia 26

Malay red harlequin butterfly (*Paralaxitta orpha*) — Southeast Asia 5

northern pintail (*Anas acuta*) — North America, Europe, Africa 10

pipistrelle bat (*Pipistrellus pipistrellus*) — Europe 19

pretty-faced or whiptail wallaby (*Macropus parryi*) — Australia 23

red-eared terrapin (*Pseudemys scripta*) — North America 16

serotine bat (*Vespertilio serotinus*) — Europe 18

springbok (*Antidorcas marsupialis*) — Southeast Asia 26

superb fairy wren (*Malarus cyaneus*) — Australia 7

tawny owl (*Strix aluco*) — Europe, Asia 23

tiger barb (*Barbus tetrazona*) — Southeast Asia 8

Books to Read

Butterflies: Magical Metamorphosis. Secrets of the Animal World (series). Eulalia Garcia (Gareth Stevens)

How Animals Protect Themselves. Animal Survival (series). Michel Barré (Gareth Stevens)

How Bats "See" in the Dark. Malcolm Penny (Benchmark Books)

Light. Science Works! (series). Steve Parker (Gareth Stevens)

The Nature and Science of Patterns. Exploring the Science of Nature (series). Jane Burton and Kim Taylor (Gareth Stevens)

Sound. Science Works! (series). Steve Parker (Gareth Stevens)

Videos and Web Sites

Videos

Color and Light. Science in Action. (TMW)
Lenses and Mirrors. Science in Action. (TMW)
National Geographic's Dolphins: The Wild Side. (National Geographic)
National Geographic's Wild Survivors: Camouflage and Mimicry. (National Geographic)

Web Sites

www.unidata.ucar.edu/staff/blynds/rnbw.html
www.opticalres.com/kidoptx.html#StartKidOptx
library.thinkquest.org/27968/kids_intro.shtml
www.geocities.com/RainForest/Vines/5983/echo.html

Some web sites stay current longer than others. For further web sites, use your search engines to locate the following topics: *camouflage, echolocation, light, mirrors, rainbows,* and *sound.*

Index